Imagining the Future

SCHOOLS

of the PAST, PRESENT, and FUTURE

Linda Bozzo

Bailey Books
an imprint of
Enslow Publishers, Inc.
40 Industrial Road
Box 398
Berkeley Heights, NJ 07922
USA
http://www.enslow.com

Bailey Books, an imprint of Enslow Publishers, Inc.

Copyright © 2011 by Enslow Publishers, Inc.

Library of Congress Cataloging-in-Publication Data

Bozzo, Linda.
    Schools of the past, present, and future / Linda Bozzo.
      p. cm. — (Imagining the future)
    Includes bibliographical references and index.
    Summary: "Look at the past, present, and future of buses, desks, clothes, learning,
      homework, writing lunch, and blackboards"—Provided by publisher.
    ISBN 978-0-7660-3434-1
    1. Schools—Juvenile literature. 2. Schools—Furniture, equipment, etc.—Juvenile
      literature. 3. Educational change—Juvenile literature. 4. Education—Effect of
      technological innovations on—Juvenile literature. I. Title.
    LB1556.B69 2011
    371—dc22
                                    2010002349

Printed in the United States of America
052010 Lake Book Manufacturing, Inc., Melrose Park, IL

10 9 8 7 6 5 4 3 2 1

Illustration Credits: ullstein bild/The Granger Collection, p. 2; Brand X Pictures/Punchstock, pp. 16 (top), 22; © ClassicStock/Alamy, pp. 14 (top), 18 (top); Kurt Gordon/iStockphoto, p. 5; Bonnie Jacobs/ iStockphoto, p. 10 (bottom); Tom LaBaff, pp. 1, 7, 9, 11, 13, 15, 17, 19, 21; Library of Congress, pp. 4, 6 (top), 20 (top); Library of Virginia, Prints and Photographs, p. 12 (top); Shutterstock, pp. 3, 6 (bottom), 8 (bottom), 10 (bottom), 12 (bottom), 14 (bottom), 16 (bottom), 18 (bottom), 20 (bottom).

Cover Illustrations: front cover—Tom LaBaff; back cover—Shutterstock.

CONTENTS

The History of School

Yesterday

School is a place where students go to learn.
At one time, not all children went to school.
Some children had to work. Other children
were needed at home.

Schools today are very different from schools one hundred years ago. Today, all children go to school or are taught at home.

Tomorrow

Have you ever wondered what schools will be like many years from now?

1. Buses

Long ago, some children rode to school in wagons pulled by horses.

Today

Today, many children ride to school on buses.

6

Imagine how children might get to school in
the **future**. Maybe they will ride in buses that
fly. That could mean getting to school faster.
Would you be able to sleep later?

2. Desks

Yesterday

At one time, desks were fixed to the floor so they could not be moved.

Today

Today, students often sit at tables or desks pushed together.

Imagine desks in the future. What if the seat was soft? Desks might come in different sizes. They might even change colors. What color desk would you choose?

3. Clothes

Yesterday

In the early 1900s, girls could only wear dresses to school. Many boys wore **knickerbockers**, pants that came just below the knee.

Today

Today, the clothes children wear to school look very different.

Tomorrow

Imagine someday wearing clothes made from **recycled** matter. Maybe clothes would stay clean without washing!

4. Learning

Yesterday

Teachers have used different machines to help students learn. Many years ago, some classrooms had film **projectors**, machines that show pictures.

Today

Today, teachers use computers to help students learn.

Tomorrow

Imagine if someday your class could visit faraway places or go back in time with the push of a button. Where would you like to go? What might you learn?

5. Homework

Yesterday

Schools once gave very little homework. Students carried their books held together with a leather strap.

Today

Today, students have more homework. Students wear backpacks to carry their books.

14

Imagine if someday students no longer carried books. Teachers might send work from their computers to your refrigerator door. What if teachers of the future did not give homework?

HOMEWORK

6. Writing

Yesterday

Long ago, students wrote with chalk on writing **slates**.

Today

Today, students write with pens and pencils on paper. They also type on computers. They print out their work on paper.

On my vacation last summer, I took a trip to Mars with my family.

Tomorrow

Imagine if in the future, you could speak to a computer and have words and pictures appear on a screen. What would you like to say?

7. Lunch

Yesterday

Children once carried their lunches to school in metal buckets or boxes.

Today

Today, some children carry their lunches to school in lunch boxes or bags. Other children buy their lunch from the school **cafeteria**.

18

Imagine if you did not have to carry your lunch to school. What if robots brought you your lunch? They might serve lunch on plates that keep your food warm or cold. What would you order?

Tomorrow

8. Blackboards

Yesterday

Teachers once wrote on slate boards and blackboards.

Today

Today, teachers write on many different types of boards, including whiteboards.

What if teachers did less writing? Instead, the lesson might come to life right before your eyes! The world we live in is always changing. Who knows what the schools of the future will look like? We can only imagine!

WORDS TO KNOW

cafeteria—A room in a school where students eat lunch.

future—The time after today.

knickerbockers—Pants for boys that came just below the knee.

projectors—Machines that use film to show still or moving pictures.

recycled—Made from material that has been used before.

slates—Small blackboards that students can hold in their hands.

LEARN MORE

Books

Ajmera, Maya, and John D. Ivanko. *Back to School.* Watertown, Mass.: Shakti for Children, 2001.

Brent, Lynette R. *At School: Long Ago and Today.* Chicago: Heinemann Library, 2003.

Nelson, Robin. *School Then and Now.* Minneapolis: Lerner Publications, 2003.

Roop, Peter and Connie. *A School Album.* Des Plaines, Ill.: Heinemann Library, 1999.

Weber, Valerie, and Gloria Jenkins. *School in Grandma's Day.* Minneapolis.: Carolrhoda Books, 1999.

Web Site

PBS Kids Go!
http://pbskids.org/wayback/future/index.html

Index